WARWICK
THE KINGMAKER
AND THE WARS OF THE ROSES

THE HELLIDON PRESS
CATESBY END, HELLIDON
NORTHAMPTONSHIRE NN11 6LG

A fateful meeting

ONE autumn morning in 1454 two men unexpectedly met in a rose garden in London. One was the Earl of Somerset, the chief counsellor to King Henry VI, and the other was the Duke of York.

Both men hated each other because they each had a claim to the throne of England and secretly hoped one day to be King. Somerset was a favourite of King Henry and his wife Queen Margaret and had great influence in governing the country. York hated Somerset and believed he was ruling the country badly and soon the two men were arguing furiously.

'Let those loyal to Lancaster wear a red rose' shouted Somerset.

'And those to York, a white rose' replied York.

Thus began a terrible and bloody civil war that divided England and was to become known as the War of the Roses. A red rose for the house of Lancaster and a white rose for the house of York. Both these two dynasties sprung from the same family – the Plantagenets.

Let battle commence

KING HENRY suffered from regular periods of madness during which his memory completely failed. He recognised no one, not even his wife Margaret, and could not understand a word that was said to him. During one of the King's illnesses, the Duke of York and his nephew, the Earl of Warwick grabbed the reins of power. They imprisoned the Earl of Somerset and for a short time governed England well. But the King recovered and immediately released Somerset from the Tower of London.

Both Warwick and York realised that they would be beheaded as traitors if they were captured. They prepared an army and marched to do battle with the King and Somerset.

The two armies met at St Albans in Hertfordshire and the first battle of the war was fought in the town. It was won by Warwick who cleverly led his men through the backstreets to attack Somerset from behind.

Somerset was killed in the fighting and there is a strange story attached to his death. When he was young, a fortune teller had told him that he would die under the walls of a castle. During the battle of St. Albans he was trapped at an Inn by Warwick's men and trying to fight his way out was fatally wounded by an axe. As he lay dying in the street he would not have been surprised to see the name of the inn – *The Castle.*

Return to peace

THE battle was won and the Yorkists were triumphant. But the King had disappeared.

When Warwick and York eventually found King Henry hiding at a cottage in the town, they knelt before him and swore allegiance. It was Somerset they had hated and he was now dead. Neither York or Warwick wanted to replace the king, but both wanted to be the power behind the throne

The King returned to London to rule as before. Despite his weaknesses, Henry was a kindly and religious man and with Warwick and York to help him govern his country all might yet have been well.

However, Queen Margaret was far from weak. Many called her a 'she wolf' because she was cruel and calculating. She hated Warwick whom she considered a traitor and was determined to have her revenge on him.

A lucky escape

ONE of Queen Margaret's plots was to lure Warwick and York to Coventry by sending them a friendly invitation to join both herself and the King there.

Not suspecting any treachery, Warwick and York set off from Warwick Castle with a small band of loyal men. As they approached the city walls, Warwick grew increasingly alarmed at the number of troops camped outside the town.

Suddenly a messenger galloped up to them. 'Flee, flee for your lives' he cried.

It was a lucky escape for had Warwick and York entered Coventry they would certainly have been cut down and killed in the narrow, cobbled city streets by the Queen's men.

King Henry knew nothing of this plot or of the seething hatred between Margaret and the Earl of Warwick. He made Warwick Captain of Calais and sent him of to France to keep the peace between the English and the French.

For several years Warwick remained in France and built up a strong fleet of ships there. But Margaret, fearing he was becoming too powerful, demanded he give up the captaincy of Calais. Warwick refused and after consulting with York again prepared for War.

At war

THERE were many minor battles and skirmishes throughout the Wars of the Roses and at first the Lancastrians got the better of it, mainly because throughout England there was a reluctance to take up arms against the King. This was because all his subjects had sworn an oath of allegiance to the crown and the fate of a traitor if caught was certain death.

The armour worn by Knights during the Wars of the Roses was very heavy. When charging on horseback, a Knight used a lance and then at close quarters he would fight with a sword or a battleaxe. He only carried a shield for jousting, never in battle because he needed both hands to wield his sword or battleaxe and because he was so well protected by his armour.

When fighting on foot a Knight was fairly clumsy, trapped by the armour that protected him. He was safe so long as the enemy were in front, but a blow from behind with an axe or a mace could stun or kill him. Also the armour could get very hot and frequently Knights were killed by arrows when they quickly took off their helmets for a breath of fresh air.

Another danger was if a Knights army was in retreat. The opposing army could rapidly overtake him, knock him to the ground, cut off his armour and either kill him or hold him to ransom. Battles were very dangerous and bloody affairs.

Escape from a battlefield

EVENTUALLY a decisive battle was fought at Northampton in 1460 and Warwick, after issuing the order that 'no man should lay hand upon the King' won a terrible victory that left the battlefield strewn with slaughtered men. King Henry was captured and escorted respectfully back to London. But Queen Margaret, furious at the defeat of her husband and still vowing for vengeance on Warwick managed to escape with her son, the Prince of Wales. She rode as hard as she could for Harlech Castle in Wales, and there she mustered another army and plotted her revenge on Warwick.

Warwick became the chief counsellor to the King and peace returned to England, when suddenly York arrived in London with a large army from Ireland and demanded the throne of England for himself. Warwick was furious. His intention had always been to keep Henry on the throne. He argued bitterly with York and then eventually reached a compromise that York should become the King when Henry died.

When Margaret heard that her own son was no longer the heir to the throne she immediately blamed Warwick and her hatred increased still further.

Advantage to Margaret

WHILE Warwick was busy in London organising a new government, Margaret moved her army to northern England. York marched north with Warwick's father, the Earl of Salisbury, to his castle near Wakefield to do battle. When Margaret's seemingly small army appeared outside the walls, York and Salisbury marched out to attack. It was a foolish mistake and they were caught in a huge ambush. Margaret had tricked them.

York was killed in the fighting and Warwick's father, Salisbury was captured and taken to Pontefract. He was later dragged out of the castle by a mob and beheaded. Warwick's young cousin, the seventeen year old Earl of Rutland was also executed.

The heads of York and Salisbury were taken to the city of York and displayed on pikes over the city gates. Margaret gave orders that a space was to be left for the head of Warwick.

Warwick assembled an army and marched to St Albans to meet Margaret's army who were heading south to London He was also tricked by Margaret who marched her troops overnight and attacked him at dawn. Warwick managed to escape from the battle and Margaret's men found the poor, confused King sitting under an oak tree from where he had observed the victory.

Warwick the Kingmaker

WARWICK's ambition had always been to be the power behind the throne which is why he had continually supported the weak King Henry, but after St Albans he came to a momentous decision. Too much blood had been spilt and too much hatred existed to ever allow King Henry to rule the country peacefully. He, Warwick, must make a new King.

He chose Edward Plantagenet, a tall and handsome young man who through birth had a good claim to the throne. On a windy March day in Westminster Abbey, Edward was crowned King. England now had two Kings.

Two days after the coronation, Warwick the Kingmaker and the new King Edward marched north. At Towton, near Tadcaster, on a very cold and grey morning two armies faced each other, both fighting for a King of England. It was to be the biggest battle ever fought on English soil.

At mid-morning snow began to fall and the wind blew it into the faces of Margaret's bowmen who could not see to aim properly. Warwick ordered the attack and throughout the day fought on foot in the thick of battle. Reinforcements arrived in the afternoon and Margaret's troops fled. Over twenty eight thousand men died during the battle.

An uneasy alliance

For the next four years England was at peace. Warwick was the real ruler in Edward's name and young Edward was happy to enjoy his position as King, but new problems for Warwick soon appeared.

Warwick wanted to ally England with France, and the best way to do this was for Edward to marry the daughter of the King of France. Whilst Warwick was negotiating this, Edward secretly married Elizabeth Woodville. Warwick was furious but did not openly quarrel with the King. But soon other arguments arose between the two men, and then insults began to fly back and forth. Most insulting of all to Warwick was having at last arranged a new alliance with France, the King refused to sign the treaty.

Bitterly Warwick retired to Warwick Castle and prepared for a new war. It was *he* who had made Edward the King and he did not want Edward to forget it. He captured Edward at Olney in Buckinghamshire and held him prisoner at Warwick Castle. Edward was treated with all deference and quickly released.

At the first opportunity, Edward declared Warwick a traitor. With no time to gather an army, Warwick and a few loyal friends were forced to flee to France with Edward's men hot on their heels.

Strange allies

For Warwick to regain power in England, he had only one option. He met with the French King and his old enemy, Queen Margaret who kept him waiting on his knees for quarter of an hour before she would forgive him. Together they planned an invasion of England with the intention of returning Henry to the throne. To seal the pact, Warwick's youngest daughter married Margaret's son, Edward, Prince of Wales.

The invasion was a complete success. As soon as Warwick landed on the south coast and unfurled his banner, the bear with the ragged staff, men came flocking. King Edward who was in the north of the country fled to King's Lynn in Norfolk. From there he took a boat to Holland. He had left in such a hurry that he had no money and the only way he could pay for his passage was by handing over his beautiful fur-lined cloak.

Henry was crowned once again but was as weak as ever. Warwick was back in power for the time being.

Tragedy in the mist

EDWARD in Holland managed to raise a small army. He landed in Yorkshire and met with an unenthusiastic reception. No-one wanted another civil war. However support grew for him as he toured the northern counties and soon he proclaimed himself King again and headed south for London.

Warwick marched to meet him and the two armies faced each other just outside London at Barnet. It was sunrise on Easter Day and a heavy mist blanketed the battlefield. The two forces were equally matched but fortune deserted Warwick. In the fog he could not control his forces and a rumour spread that they were losing the battle. Reinforcements arrived from Barnet but were mistaken for the enemy and soon Warwick's army were fighting not only Edward's troops but each other.

Warwick realised he had lost the day. He hurried as quickly as his heavy armour would allow to find his horse, fighting as he went. But it was no good. In the confusion, the panic and the mist, the great Earl of Warwick was killed.

ACKNOWLEDGEMENTS

The publishers would like to thank Ladybird Books for permission to reproduce all the colour illustrations in this book. Also we are indebted to the staff at Warwick Castle for their willing assistance in the preparation of this book.

Produced by the Hellidon Press. 01327 263852